NATURAL **DISASTERS**

LANDSLIDES

ABDO
Publishing Company

Rochelle Baltzer

Big Buddy **BOOKS**
Natural Disasters

VISIT US AT
www.abdopublishing.com

Published by ABDO Publishing Company, 8000 West 78th Street, Edina, Minnesota 55439.

Printed in the United States of America, North Mankato, Minnesota.
052011
092011
 PRINTED ON RECYCLED PAPER

Coordinating Series Editor: Sarah Tieck
Contributing Editors: Megan M. Gunderson, BreAnn Rumsch, Marcia Zappa
Graphic Design: Adam Craven
Cover Photograph: *AP Photo*: Nick Ut.
Interior Photographs/Illustrations: *AP Photo*: Darryl Dyck/The Canadian Press (p. 11), Saieb Haddad/Tennessee
    Department of Transportation (p. 21), Jebb Harris, Pool (pp. 15, 17), Imaginechina via AP Images (pp. 25, 27),
    Virginia Mayo, File (p. 7), Phil McCarten (p. 17), Pat Rogue (p. 5), Mark J. Terrill (p. 15); *Getty Images*: Stephen
    Brashear (p. 23), JAY DIRECTO/AFP (p. 23), Dr. Marli Miller (p. 9), Joseph Baylor Roberts (p. 19); *Photo
    Researchers, Inc.*: Science Source/USGS (p. 30); *Photolibrary*: Bios (p. 11), Lineair (p. 11), Loop Images (p. 13),
    Robert Harding Travel (p. 29); *Shutterstock*: robootb (p. 25).

Library of Congress Cataloging-in-Publication Data

Baltzer, Rochelle, 1982-
  Landslides / Rochelle Baltzer.
    p. cm. -- (Natural disasters)
  ISBN 978-1-61783-033-4
  1. Landslides--Juvenile literature. I. Title.
  QE599.A2B35 2011
  363.34'9--dc22
                            2011013146

LANDSLIDES

CONTENTS

POWERFUL LANDSLIDES

Rain pounds down on a steep hillside. The ground becomes muddy. Loose soil on the hill moves down. More and more slips, covering plants and rocks. It's a landslide!

A landslide is a natural disaster. Natural disasters happen because of weather or changes inside Earth. They can cause much **damage** and even take lives. By learning about them, people are better able to stay safe.

Landslides can destroy cities and natural areas.

BREAKING NEWS

Landslides can be wet or dry. Some kinds of wet landslides are also called mudslides or mudflows.

GETTING DOWN

A landslide is a mass of soil or rock that moves down a slope. Some landslides move very fast. Others move slow over many years.

BREAKING NEWS

An avalanche (A-vuh-lanch) is like a landslide. It is a mass of snow that moves down a mountain.

The fastest landslides can move more than 15 feet (5 m) per second!

LOOK OUT BELOW!

Landslides happen around the world. They often occur in places with lots of hills or mountains. They are also common in areas that have **earthquakes** or **volcanoes**.

Landslides can even happen underwater! On the ocean floor, it is called a submarine landslide. This can lead to a **tsunami**.

Landslides are most common in mountains and near coasts.

SLIP SLIDING AWAY

Common types of landslides include slides, falls, and flows. In a slide, a weak **layer** of rock and soil slides down. It moves over a stronger layer of ground.

In a fall, a chunk of rock suddenly separates from connecting rock. It falls or rolls to lower ground.

A flow is when soil and rock mix with water. Together, they move as if they are liquid. They flow down and out, covering land.

slide

fall

flow

11

CAUSE AND EFFECT

Landslides occur on slopes where land is weak. Land becomes weak when soil or rock loosens. A force called **gravity** pulls the loosened parts down.

Certain events can start a landslide. Heavy rain or fast-melting snow turns loose soil into a muddy liquid. **Earthquakes** can cause loose rock to move. As rock and soil slip, a landslide begins.

Some types of rock are naturally weaker than others. This makes landslides more likely.

13

Some natural changes make areas more likely to have a landslide. For example, **erosion** can make slopes very steep. And, wildfires burn down plants and trees that help hold soil in place.

Human activities can also lead to landslides. Removing trees for building makes land weak. Building too many homes on slopes can also weaken land.

In 2003, parts of California had mudslides after heavy rain (*above*). Wildfires had burned areas (*right*), making landslides more likely.

RESCUE ME!

Not all landslides cause heavy **damage**. But a fast, powerful landslide plows through land. It picks up and moves objects in its path. This includes trees, cars, and even people and animals. **Debris** can bury roads and homes.

After a landslide, workers **rescue** people. Cleanup workers clear away debris. Communities work together to rebuild areas.

Rescue workers search for trapped people.

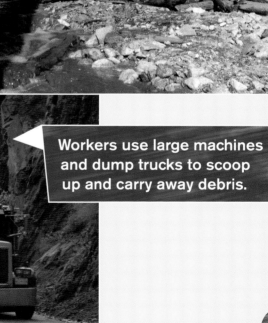

Workers use large machines and dump trucks to scoop up and carry away debris.

CHANGING THE EARTH

Landslides change Earth's surface. They wipe away the sides of hills and mountains. This can make an area look much different.

If a landslide occurs near a river, it can cause a dam. Rock and soil slide down and build up in the river. This blocks the river from flowing, which can lead to floods. Sometimes, this even creates a lake!

In 1959, a large earthquake caused a landslide in Montana. About 80 million tons (73 million t) of rock made a dam in the Madison River.

STAYING SAFE

In places where landslides are likely, people watch for warning signs. They look for leaning trees or fences and cracks in the ground. These signs may mean ground is not stable.

People listen to the radio or television for warnings of heavy rain. They may need to leave their homes to stay safe.

BREAKING NEWS

Landslides can happen weeks or months after a big storm. So, people keep watching for warning signs.

In some places, special walls are built at the bottom of slopes. These reduce harm from landslides.

21

STUDYING LANDSLIDES

Scientists study landslides. They look at how and when they happen. They measure slopes and study soil and rock. They learn where land is weak. Their work helps people be better prepared.

The US Geological Survey works on ways to see early landslide warning signs. Then, officials can warn people in the area.

Some scientists study earth and rock. They spend time outside to learn about landslides.

CASE STUDY:
GANSU LANDSLIDE

In summer 2010, heavy rain caused **severe** floods in parts of China. The extra water made the land weak. Landslides were likely to happen.

On August 8, a landslide moved downhill into a town in Gansu Province. Mud and **debris** swept away cars and buried homes. Many people were killed or trapped.

The Gansu landslide destroyed thousands of homes.

MONGOLIA

CHINA

GANSU PROVINCE

Area of Landslide

Rescue workers searched for missing people. They brought more than 1,000 people to safety. Still, more than 1,000 others died.

In China, people remembered those affected by the landslide on August 15. Flags flew at half-mast. And, public activities, such as movies, were closed.

A major landslide can make water dirty. This makes it easier for people to get sick.

Many people lost their homes in the landslide. So, they lived in tents for a while. They were given food, bottled water, and blankets.

27

FORCE OF NATURE

Landslides are powerful. They change Earth's surface. And, they can cause much **damage**.

Landslides will always happen. But the more people learn about them, the more prepared they can be. This saves lives!

Landslides can damage homes built on weak ground on hills. People work to learn the safest places to build homes.

NEWS FLASH!

- The slowest landslides move less than one inch (2.5 cm) per year.

- Scientists say the largest landslide may have taken place billions of years ago on Mars. It was the size of the United States!

- In the United States, landslides kill about 25 to 50 people every year. Many more die in landslides around the world.

- The largest recorded landslide happened in 1980 at Mount Saint Helens in Washington. It left behind enough **debris** to fill more than 250 million dump trucks!

IMPORTANT WORDS

damage (DA-mihj) harm or injury.

debris (duh-BREE) bits and pieces of something broken down or wrecked.

earthquake (UHRTH-kwayk) a shaking of a part of the earth.

erosion (ih-ROH-zhuhn) wearing away of the land often caused by water or wind.

gravity a natural force that pulls objects downward.

layer a part that is on top of or underneath another part.

rescue (REHS-kyoo) to save from danger or harm.

severe (suh-VIHR) causing danger, hardship, or pain.

tsunami (soo-NAH-mee) a group of powerful ocean waves that can destroy areas.

volcano a deep opening, or vent, in Earth's surface from which hot liquid rock or steam comes out.

WEB SITES

To learn more about landslides, visit ABDO Publishing Company online. Web sites about landslides are featured on our Book Links page. These links are routinely monitored and updated to provide the most current information available.

www.abdopublishing.com

INDEX